Happy Mealtimes with Happy Kids:

How to Teach Your Child About the Joy of Food!

Practical and Surprising Tips from a Pediatric Feeding Specialist

Melanie Potock, MA, CCC-SLP

Published by: My Munch Bug Publishing
Box 382
Longmont, CO 80502
www.mymunchbug.com

ISBN   978-0-557-60655-9

Dedication and Acknowledgements

I am not quite sure where to begin, as I have had the good fortune of being supported in this journey by so many friends and family. To Aimee, Cheryl, Marika, Rachel and Shannon: How lucky I was to have met five fabulous moms who welcomed me into their homes with open arms and answered many a late-night email with kindness and superb guidance. To Michelle, for painstakingly editing every single page and when I asked how I could repay her graciously answered,

"The only thing I would really like is a big boy who can eat with gusto and joy... oh, wait, I have one now! We're thankful every day for the fun and relaxed way in which you taught us how to help our son and helped him get to the point where he can go anywhere and eat anything... "

Thank you to my daughter Mallory, for teaching me to keep a straight face when as a toddler, she loved to order "Seizure Salad" at restaurants. Thank you to my youngest daughter, Carly, for being my picky eater, which started me thinking: "Is cereal and milk for dinner really worth stressing about?" Most of all, my heart goes out to my sweet husband, who truly believed in me and supported my dream of being an author. Thank you, thank you, thank you...this book is dedicated to all of you with love and gratitude.

Contents

Introduction

White Gloves and Party Manners

When I was 10 years old, my well-intentioned parents signed me up for charm school. Yes, charm school. Mortified, I was dressed in my best party getup and dropped off at a very fancy class in Denver for three miserable hours every single, precious Saturday for six painful, no excruciating weeks. Get the picture?

Each session was devoted to the essentials that every little girl should know, including how to properly wrap your freshly shampooed hair in a towel-turban (with the final edge tucked immaculately into the center fold), how to fold your legs just so — at the ankles and tilted at the proper angle under your chair, skirt over your knees, hands folded as if you were delicately holding an invisible cup and saucer (never, ever fingers intertwined!) and resting in your lap. Most importantly, I learned how to wear white gloves to a birthday party and which fork to use when eating the salad or later, when eating the cake. Because, as we all know, white gloves and salad are staples at most children's birthday parties. I also learned how to curtsy, should I ever meet the queen. Still waiting on that one.

It's possible that out of revenge, I became a feeding therapist. Feeding therapy is all about getting messy with food and, frankly, white gloves and party manners are not. Oh, I can still quite skillfully choose the correct fork and sure, I taught my own two daughters to wrap a darn good turban, but my daily life is about having fun with food.

My own mother, who admirably used to put the catsup in a tiny ceramic dish rather than putting the plastic bottle on the dinner table, is still not quite sure what a 'feeding therapist" does, but she knows I teach kids to eat healthy foods, which is what every mom can appreciate. So, my white gloves have been replaced with purple latex ones and the party may look more like a food fight, but in the end, we get to eat salad and cake too, and even get cake in our hair, which is where the towel turban can really come in handy.

So, in the end, it worked out perfectly, because I grew up to have the best job in the world! I play with little kids all day long, eat all day long and never stop laughing because my job is just way too much fun! The parents I work with are true gems — they know that we are a team and that we all want their children to enjoy a variety of nutritious foods, so together we take it step-by-step on our destination to healthy, independent eating!

Thanks for listening to my story. Now, on to the best part of this book: your little sweetheart. This book is all about mealtimes and your adorable little munch bug: It's filled with useful tips that every parent should know when it comes to teaching kids the joy of food. This book is meant to make life easier and mealtimes happier, for both you and your child!

I purposely kept this book short, as I know that parents of young children rarely get time to read more than a few pages before duties call! Thus, each chapter has an appetizer, an entree and a quick bite. The appetizers are snippets of my life as a feeding therapist; the entree offers more "meat" on the chapter's topic and, finally, the quick bite is what most parents and caregivers truly have time for — a speedy synopsis of the tips offered in each chapter.

Please keep in mind that this is not a rulebook, it's a guidebook. Children have many different reasons for having trouble eating, and that is where your pediatrician and a speech therapist or an occupational therapist who specializes in feeding can be your best resource. But, it is my hope for you that this book will provide a basic foundation for any new parent, any mom or dad who is searching for answers to their child's idiosyncrasies about food and for my favorite parent of all — the one who says "Maybe I should glance through that book... I might learn something new!" Have fun and happy eating!

Melanie

(a.k.a. Lemony, Mennanie, Nemalie, Mimi, Watermelon and/or Miss Mel)

A Note for Parents of Children Currently in Feeding Therapy or Who May Have Special Needs

When I first became a speech language pathologist specializing in feeding, I recommended my usual regimen of well-known books about "picky eating" to new families, offering access to my personal library whenever they needed it. "Have you read _____?" I would ask. One very honest mom who taught me many lessons over the years replied, "Yes, and after I read it cover to cover, I threw it across the room. That author didn't have a clue what my family was going through." She was right — none of us have a complete understanding of each child's exceptional needs and the impact those issues have on their family. I will never forget that moment and am so grateful for the excellent education that mom gave to me.

Every child is unique - especially when it comes to children who have difficulty eating. My hope is that as a parent or caregiver of a child with special needs, you will approach the information in this book as a baseline. This guidance is intended as the fundamentals of what I would like every parent of any child to know. It's merely a start. Only a professional can support you through the next steps via regular therapy visits. You may also notice that it doesn't have a lot of "therapy" strategies. Individual therapy is best left up to the individual therapist treating the individual child.

However, should you like more detailed information regarding therapy treatments and oral motor strategies, please refer to the resources listed at the end of this book. Thank you for reading my book, and please write to me at www.MyMunchBug.com. I value your input!

Chapter One

What a Position to Be In!

Proper Positioning in the Feeding Chair

Can you picture this? Adorable curly-head moppet named Megan, a feisty 13-month-old, seated in her very fancy designer high chair, ready for her first session of feeding therapy! Dad has lovingly begun to feed her a little of her favorite mush as I get settled in to observe. There she was, tilted way, way back in her personal toddler-sized La-Z-Boy® recliner looking as happy as my husband on Super Bowl Sunday. I almost handed her a beer and the remote. As her dad proudly brought the bright blue spoon to her mouth she eagerly shifted her position to try and reach it: weight on her seat bones and... ugh! So hard to get up! Get those tiny toes up in the air... Make them peek over the high chair tray... Can you see 'em? Yes! Lift those shoulders, just enough to make those "abs" contract...Don't forget to point your chin to the sky! Raise up the arms to salute the sun... Wait, are we in toddler yoga or just trying to eat pureed carrots? Megan continued to salute the sun with every bite, happily smiling at her Daddy until she

just couldn't lift her little arms and toes any more.
It's hard to do yoga and eat at the same time.

The first step to learning to eat solids, even purees, is correct positioning in the feeding chair. Only babies who cannot yet sit up on their own and are ready to start smooth purees can sit back at a slight angle in a high chair or booster seat, providing that it is intended to recline.

Be sure that your child is supported at her hips and below so that her hips don't slide forward and cause her to slump. Therapists love to use a piece of shelf liner — the spongy, waffle weave kind that you can buy at the dollar store in a little roll. Sitting on shelf liner provides a low-slip surface that grips little bottoms better than anything I know! Parents can also roll the liner into small bolsters to provide trunk support as needed. One long rolled-up piece can be placed under the child's knees for stability and to help keep his back against the high chair. Be sure that the shelf liner doesn't interfere with the safety straps on the booster or high chair and always use the straps to secure your child.

Once your little one is sitting up with some support and is transitioning to independent eating, it's time to end the La-Z-Boy® days. Independent eating refers to the child's emerging ability to pick up food with her fingers and begin sloppily yet adorably using a spoon on her own. You may find that she needs some support around her trunk once you raise the seat to approximately 90 degrees.

The child should be sitting up straight, with the top of the high chair tray at the bottom of the breastbone. Hips, knees and ankles are at a 90 degree angle. It is very important for stability to provide her with something to rest her feet on. Try sitting on a high bar stool while having a snack and let your feet dangle — it's tiring! Most high chairs come with a foot rest, but may need a long, narrow cardboard box (like a Saltine box) duct taped to the foot rest to bring the "rest" up to the heels of the feet. With a booster seat, sometimes just the breadth of the adult chair provides a little extra ledge for tiny heels and toes to rest upon. One creative parent I know duct taped phone books together under her child's chair so that she had a stable resting place for her sneakers.

As your child grows, the same rules apply. Ninety degree angle at hips and knees, table top at the bottom of the breastbone and sweet little feet supported.

When your child can sit upright with some support:

- Hips, knees and ankles should be at a 90 degree angle.
- Keep the table top or tray level with the bottom of the breastbone.
- Allow flat feet to rest on a support.

Chapter Two

"Like, Gag Me with a Spoon!"

Knowing Which Spoon to Use and How to Use It

Spoons... they are so complicated! Have you ever walked down the baby aisle and seen the enormous selection of feeding tools? Short handles, long handles, curved handles, bumpy handles... big bowls, double bowls, bowls with holes, I do not like these bowls! Oh no, I am starting to sound like Dr. Seuss!

Correct spoon feeding is actually a very important skill! Sure, the difference in spoon shape, size and texture is probably a bit of marketing, but it is also quite valuable to understand how it relates to your child's development.

When introducing the spoon for the first time, choose a spoon that has a fairly small bowl so that it will not overwhelm your baby's tiny mouth. A more flat bowl at this stage of the game will help your baby learn to use her upper lip to clean the food from the spoon efficiently and effectively. A spoon that has a coated or slightly flexible bowl may offer a gentler touch for those first tries or for babies who are cutting teeth.

Once your child is supported correctly in her feeding chair, be sure to adjust your positioning so that you are directly in front of her and at her eye level. Eye contact and engaging with your child during mealtimes is the foundation for success because this is a shared, social occasion. From a social perspective, sit across from your child so that you are at eye level and enjoy each other's company! From a technical perspective, this position allows your hand and the spoon it holds to be presented at the child's mouth at the perfect angle. Correct hand placement encourages your child to look straight ahead, rather than up. Babies who tilt their heads up during feedings are at risk for aspiration, or food going into their lungs. Therapists discourage "bird feeding" because it promotes incorrect motor patterns of the tongue, lips and jaw, including tongue thrusting past the age of six months.

All infants are born with a reflex known as the tongue thrust reflex. You may have noticed that when you touch an infant's lips, her tongue automatically or reflexively moves forward toward the stimulation. This reflex typically fades or integrates at about four months of age. Today, the American Academy of Pediatrics recommends offering your baby solid foods between four and six months of age, so you may see your baby try to expel the spoon by pushing it away with her tongue if the reflex is still present, and she may not be ready for solid foods. Once the tongue thrust has faded, therapists do not want to encourage a more exaggerated version of this motor pattern to develop. Tongue thrusting can become a "life long pattern that is known to affect the development and shape of the hard palate (the roof of the mouth) and teeth" according to Diane Bahr, MS, CCC-SLP, a nationally known expert on feeding and oral motor skills. (1)

Many pediatricians recommend starting solids by mixing rice cereal with warm breast milk, liquid formula or water to form a thin puree. It is often helpful to dip the tip of the spoon in the puree and let your baby have a first taste. Likewise, help your child become accustomed to the spoon by helping her hold it and mouth it — but if the spoon has a long handle, watch carefully that she holds the handle close to the bowl so that she doesn't accidentally hurt herself.

Once she has become accustomed to the new taste and pureed texture, present the spoon in front of the baby's lips and wait for her to open her mouth. Be sure that the small bowl of the spoon is only ¼ to ½ full so that the amount of food, or bolus, is not overwhelming. Place the spoon in her mouth and watch for her jaw to close before slowly removing the spoon. As her skill improves, her top lip will also close over the spoon in order to clear the bowl of puree.

One popular technique passed down over generations is the "tilt and scrape". When the child's jaw closes down on the spoon, the feeder elevates her hand and tilts the handle tip upward while the food is scraped onto the hard palate (or behind the front teeth if the baby has teeth) as the spoon is removed from the baby's mouth. The problem with this age-old (and flawed) technique is that the child's tongue immediately elevates to find the puree and then thrusts forward to remove it. As the tongue thrusts, the puree is scraped to the middle of the tongue to be swallowed. This method is also typical of a caregiver who is in a rush. Allow your child sufficient time to learn to accept the spoon, close the jaw and lips and clean the spoon on her own as you slowly remove it. Her skills will improve quite rapidly thanks to your patience and steady guidance.

For more detailed information on how a baby's mouth and face develop for feeding and speech, please refer to Diane Bahr's book *Nobody Ever*

Told Me (or My Mother) That! listed in the resources at the end of this book.

When your baby is learning to eat purees:

- Feed eye-to-eye so your baby does not have to look up.
- Use a baby spoon with a small bowl only partially filled with puree.
- Place at least half the spoon in her mouth and wait.
- When her jaw closes, slowly remove the spoon.
- Over time, she will also rest her top lip on the spoon to clear the puree. Wait for her lip to rest on the spoon and then remove.

Chapter Three

I Can Do it Myself!

Messy Steps to Self Feeding

Isaac's grandmother diligently swiped his chin with the tip of the spoon after every bite, ensuring that no puree remained on his face. She kept a wet washcloth nearby for swiftly wiping down soiled fingers and the high chair tray should any food drip off the spoon. "He likes to be neat and clean," she stated proudly. Isaac was 18-months-old and had yet to touch a spoon or any food on his tray. Thankfully, this grandmother was open to my suggestions and, months later, Isaac, Grandma and I were elbow-deep in chocolate as we played pudding car wash on his back patio! That grandmother later told me: "If you haven't played pudding car wash, you're missing out on life!"

I always turn my radar up a bit when I see a one-year-old sitting in his high chair, being fed by his parent and spotless — not a mess under the high chair, not a stain on his bib, not a speck on his tray. Well-meaning parents try to spare their child (and themselves) the mess by continuing to spoon feed their little one. Not only is the mess part of the learning curve for self feeding, it's essential for children to encounter the sensory experience of each and every food. Many children need to first explore new foods with their eyes, ears, nose and hands before putting it in their mouths. Please refer to Chapter 4 for more information on sensory experiences with food.

Once your child is sitting on her own or with a bit of support and you have her properly positioned in her high chair (see Chapter 1), she is ready to begin more independent feeding. This stage of the game is all about you providing a variety of safe foods for her to try, engaging with her as she eats and letting her get messy as she explores all of the new foods.

Self spoon feeding is an art. You can support your child by encouraging her to hold the handle of the spoon fairly close to the bowl. This varies depending on the shape of the handle, but, in general, the closer her little fist is to the bowl, the easier she will be able to guide the bowl into her mouth with less mess. Keep in mind that the closer her fist is to the bowl, the messier her hand will get when she scoops up that first spoonful of applesauce!

Try coloring a wide circle around the handle with a permanent marker so that she has a consistent spot to aim for when she grasps the handle. Pick a spot for her grasp about one inch from the bowl, or, if the handle is curved, have her grasp it at the top of the curve. A short, fat handle with a curve or "hill" built into the handle is often ideal. The deeper bowl will hold the puree or chopped food as it travels the long trek up to your child's mouth, but the child may not be able to clean the spoon with his top lip as easily.

Some spoons come with holes in the bowl to allow liquid to drain and solids to stick to the bowl. Other spoons have textured bowls for those children who need the added tactile input to their mouths in order to tell where the spoon is about to dump the food. Some spoons come with bendable "necks" where the handle and the bowl meet, so that parents can adjust the angle of the neck to facilitate better hand to mouth coordination.

Provide extra traction beneath the slippery bowl with a sheet of shelf liner (see Chapter 1) or use a suction cup bowl. Suction cup bowls that are deep with high sides are ideal, especially if filled with non-slippery foods such as cottage cheese, oatmeal or chopped, room temperature macaroni and cheese.

I am not sure which is messier — independent spoon feeding or independent finger feeding! A washable mat under the high chair tray is a must. Finger feeding is the perfect opportunity for your little foodie to begin to develop his pincer grasp, where he engages his thumb and forefinger to pick up pea-sized foods, such as halved blueberries and cheerios.

At about six months, your child will begin to rake up objects by using his whole hand and curling all four fingers around the desired item. Letting go of the food can be tricky. You may see your child use his mouth to grab the food while he fists it in between his little fingers.

Slowly, between seven and nine months, the pincer grasp will begin to emerge. This is also the time that children have enough trunk stability to sit in a high chair and focus on this new skill. Typically, by the end of the first year, the pincer grasp is perfected! At that time, you will see your child begin to pick up small pieces of food and place them in her mouth with more precision and thankfully, less mess.

Support the natural progression of finger feeding by offering soft or meltable foods first, such as a buttery cracker. It's relatively easy to grasp and mouth until a soft, mushy piece falls into his mouth. Over time, he will develop his ability to grade his jaw movement and truly bite into the cracker in a controlled, even manner. As his skills improve, offer pea-sized pieces of soft and/or meltable foods that expose your child to a variety of tastes, safe temperatures and textures. Small chilly blueberries cut in half, warm, buttery pieces of pasta or tofu or cheerios spritzed with apple juice are all good starters. See Chapter 15 for additional ideas.

To encourage pincer grasp development, try the following games with your favorite round cereal or pea-sized pieces of soft food:

1. Using a plastic "shot glass" or similar sized narrow container (about two inches tall and just wide enough for your child's thumb and forefinger), put a few pieces of cereal in the bottom and encourage him to get them out by reaching in and picking up the pieces using a pincer grasp.

2. Take a round plastic coffee stirrer and thread three pieces of circular cereal on it.

Hold it perpendicular to the high chair tray and let your child pull off the cereal one by one using his thumb and forefinger.

3. When giving your child a piece of the cereal, hold it in your pincer grasp (with half sticking out and available for his little fingers to grab onto) as you move it toward his hand. Wait. Let him take it from your grasp before putting it in his mouth on his own.

As your child learns to feed himself with fingers and/or spoon:

- Rejoice in the mess! It's good for his sensory system and just part of the learning curve.
- Position little fists near the bowl of the spoon.
- Layer shelf liner under a small, deep plastic bowl or use a suction cup bowl.
- Offer pea-sized soft and/or meltable foods to encourage pincer grasp.

Chapter Four

Young Explorers

Experiencing Temperature and Texture

Before Taste

I recently received the following email from a wonderful mom who recounted her daughter's need to explore foods with her entire sensory system before putting them in her mouth. She was having trouble gaining weight — and it all came down to a hypersensitive gag reflex that made eating an unpredictable and scary experience. We began working together when Katie had just turned two-years-old.

Dear Mel,

When John and I tried to give Katie "big girl food" she played with it. It wasn't normal play; she spent much time rolling blueberries along her legs, string cheese up and down her cheeks and mashing bananas in her hands. John and I got most frustrated when she took yogurt and basically painted her body with it. At first, we lost our patience and took away the food. We tried to get her to stop "playing" with her food and just eat it! It occurred again and again. It was only later after you taught us about the hierarchy of eating and respecting her entire sensory system that it clicked! She wasn't avoiding eating, she was experiencing it.

This epiphany happened one morning as she painted yogurt on her face and along her legs; (CLICK!!) She never experienced food like most babies! Because she never ate baby food (not from our lack of trying) she didn't have the opportunity to get messy. She didn't experience the slimy, wet feel on her hands or face as most babies do as their parents spoon feed them pureed food or as they learn to spoon feed themselves. This was a step in the hierarchy that she skipped. I realized she needed to experience foods as a baby would experience food. From that point on, we allowed her to roll food along arms, legs and face as well as paint her body with yogurt. Her confidence in trying new foods started to blossom with this new freedom. As parents we "let go" and knew her actions were purposeful. Slowly, as she developed an awareness of these new foods, instead of ending up all over her body, they found their way inside her mouth!

She still rolls and mashes occasionally, but the body paint is a thing of the past. As parents, we no longer feel the constant frustration; instead, we try to provide the positive eating environment she needs to feel confident and enjoy food. We have all come a long way!

Over 40 years ago, Dr. A. Jean Ayres, an occupational therapist and outstanding researcher, introduced the theory of sensory integration, or the study of how the brain processes information from our entire sensory system. A multitude of sensory input flows into the brain to be sorted and organized. Which signal is important? Which input can be discarded at this time? Which is the most important piece of information that applies to what I am doing at this very moment? It requires a very well-organized brain to answer each question efficiently and effectively and the entire process is nothing short of amazing.

"Sensory integration puts it all together. Imagine peeling and eating an orange. You sense the orange through your eyes, nose, mouth, the skin on your hands and fingers, and also the muscles and joints inside your fingers, hands, arms, and mouth… All the sensations from the orange and all the sensations from your hands and fingers somehow come together in one place in your brain" which allows you to make decisions on how to peel and eat the orange. (2)

For many individuals, automatically integrating the various levels of sensations is not always easy. Katie's parents recognized that their very bright child was resisting eating because she needed to experience all aspects of temperature and texture prior to taste. Katie experienced these through her entire body via tactile input, visual input, auditory input (yes, each food has its own sound!)

and smell. Katie's vestibular system, which is a function of the inner ear, also went to work as she moved her head to roll the food up and down her legs. As her muscles contracted and stretched with each mash of banana on her arms, her brain received proprioceptive input to tell her brain exactly what her hands were doing. For more detailed information on the fascinating topic of sensory integration, please refer to *Sensory Integration and the Child* by A. Jean Ayres, PhD or Dr. Lucy Jane Miller's book, *Sensational Kids: Hope and Help for Children with Sensory Processing Disorder.*

Katie's mother and I discussed at length approaching Katie's exploration of each food as a hierarchy — step by step. Can she tolerate that particular food on her high chair tray without gagging? Can she touch it without gagging? Can she pick it up, touch it to her body and eventually to her lips? Will she kiss it? How about a big long smooch or is it a quick peck? Can she tap dance across her pearly whites with it? Can she hold it on her molars (we like to call those Tyrannosaurus Teeth!) or does she need to hold it on her front teeth or "the front door of her mouth house" for a while? For Katie, gagging got in the way of sprinting to the top of the eating staircase.

She had to take it step by step and sometimes, she just hung out on a step for a while and mashed and smushed her food until she had learned enough about it to move to the next stair on the hierarchy. Occasionally, if her sensory system wasn't in top form that day, she would take a step down and experience the food in a simpler manner, such as just looking at it on her plate. The next day, she would typically move back up the stairs by first touching it, picking it up and possibly even smashing it onto her tray. Think about it: a roly-poly pea is a whole different vegetable when it's smashed. Now it is just mush and pea skin! YUM! Time to start at the bottom stair and work our way up to eating this brand new food... wonder what happened to that roly-poly pea?

Children need to experience food via their entire sensory system. Food play is an important component to learning about texture, temperature and taste! In addition to cooking together, use food for:

- building blocks (e.g. carrot chips; crouton cubes)

- messy, sensory play (e.g. pudding paint)

- board games (e.g. zucchini slices instead of checkers)

- pretend play (e.g. teddy bear crackers on fruit leather beds - "Ni- night Teddy!"

Chapter Five

Ice Cream is NOT Ice Cream

When It's Melted... It's Soup!

How Children Learn To Tolerate Change

Jackson sat in his high chair, suspiciously eyeing the ice cream fudge bar that his mother had set on his tray. He tried to pick up the icy chocolate with his little fist and dropped it immediately. Not wanting to get too close to the sting of the frozen treat, he used his pincer grasp to grab the end of the stick and just couldn't lift the top-heavy fudge bar... so he studied it. He pushed it with one finger across the tray creating a thin river of melted chocolate ice cream. Aha! Here was something he recognized: chocolate milk! Jackson bent over the tray, stuck out his tongue and lapped away!

Change is hard. Even for adults, very few of us like to jump into new circumstances without first assessing the situation and making mental notes as to how to proceed. Kids are like that, too, when it comes to food, especially food that changes over time, like ice cream. It starts out rock hard, biting cold and a bit frosty and in a very short amount of time is creamy, room temperature soup! Tortillas with cheese are another yummy example; soft and pliable one second and rubbery the next. Many parents comment to me that their little one will "only eat it when it's a little warm and a little soft." Problem is, that stage of the cheese tortilla is just a moment in time!

When serving your child a food that will change in taste, temperature and/or texture while on his plate, keep the servings small — two tablespoons or two servings the size of a fifty-cent piece. Keep the second helpings in the oven or the refrigerator so that they are served in a consistent manner until your child adjusts to the change over time.

To help your sweet munchkin learn to tolerate the changes, get creative with your language. As parents focused on safety, we often teach our children "hot" first and foremost. Now try words that describe the transformation in the food, such as melty, sticky, stringy, tender, gooey, soupy or just drip, drip, drip! For example, when eating tortillas with cheese, try phrases such as "Yum, now it's nice and stringy! WOW! Look how long the cheese stretches!" or "My tortilla isn't stringy anymore, so my teeth are going to BITE a happy smile right into it!" Kids will learn to tolerate changes in food if parents model how to adapt to the food as temperature and texture vary over time. As adults, we know how to grade our bite so that our teeth settle "just so" into the gooey cheese spilling between the sheets of tortilla. Toddlers, on the other hand, are experiencing this for the first time. Use direct teaching and show them how to hold the tortilla or the stick of the ice cream bar. This is all new territory for them and kids gain confidence when they have a guide through this new adventure!

Many foods require gradual exposure. For one little girl whom I adored, eating anything straight out of the freezer was tortuous. She just couldn't handle the sudden shock of icy cold foods. Once she learned how to hold a popsicle by the stick, we practiced dunking it into a tall glass of water. As she pulled the popsicle from its bath, the water clung to the sides and she licked it off. She was fascinated by the orange swirls of popsicle "juice" in the water and eventually was sucking on the popsicle as she dipped and tasted, dipped and tasted. Biting into the solid pop required more practice over a few sessions. Before we knew it, popsicles straight from the freezer became her new favorite delicacy!

Thrilled with her new success, her parents offered her ice cream — and, you guessed it, she refused! Ice cream and popsicles are two totally different foods. Hmmm... how to bridge the difference? What's frozen and shaped like a popsicle? A fudge bar. Eureka! For this little girl, dipping the fudge bar wasn't necessary — it was similar enough to a popsicle. But, if she needed it, we would have given that fudge bar a nice bath of cool water before we had a taste! Now, when is a fudge bar more like a bowl of ice cream? When you give her a plastic knife and a bowl and teach her to hold onto the stick, cut pieces off the end, and eat it with a spoon. When is a cut-up fudge bar more like a bowl of chocolate milk? When you stir it up (don't forget to make the motor boat noise —this is essential to the success of the recipe!) round and round and round and presto chango, chocolate M! Now keep stirring until you warm it up a bit... and you have chocolate soup. Tomorrow night, bring out a few small scoops of ice cream, about the size of two 50-cent pieces. Let her experiment. Let her experience the change on her own terms. Let her decide when to taste it. Don't forget to have your own bowl and ice cream as you talk about the transition from ice cream to soup. Change is best tackled gradually; then it doesn't feel like change at all.

To help your child tolerate the changes in temperature, texture and, consequently, taste:

- Offer two small, 50-cent sized portions to limit the time it sits on her plate.
- Use direct teaching ("hold the stick like this").
- Use language that describes the changes such as gooey, stretchy, melty.

Chapter Six

Straw Drinking 101

It's Easier Than You Think!

One lovely Colorado afternoon, I sat along a sidewalk patio restaurant with a mom and dad and their sweet nine-month-old daughter, Sadie. We were enjoying some time together over a light lunch as shoppers strolled by along the outdoor mall. Sadie's mom reached over to her water glass and offered Sadie a drink from her straw. Sadie took a quick sip and made a silly face when the cold water touched her tongue. Giggles erupted and the people passing by couldn't help but notice the four of us having so much fun!

Sadie continued to sip on the straw and one woman stopped to ask "How old? She's so cute!"

Dad jumped in, quite proud and announced, "She's nine-months-old!"

"And she's drinking from a straw?" the woman asked, clearly surprised.

"Oh, she's been doing that since seven months. We skipped the sippy cup. Straws are so good for their oral motor development, you know." I almost jumped up and hugged him, I was so pleased with Sadie's dad! He gave me a wink, his wife started to laugh at my proud expression and little Sadie just kept sipping away!

Every child in my practice learns to drink from a straw at the earliest age possible for their level of oral motor skill. Straw drinking is like weight lifting — it creates stronger oral musculature and improves stability during movement of the oral structures, including the lips, tongue and jaw that are essential for eating solids and for talking. Think about the last time you had a fruit-filled smoothie or thick milk shake... remember that tired feeling in the back of your tongue? It's hard work!

Here's the lickety-split, super quick run down of basic tongue anatomy. Your tongue has laterally symmetrical muscles with a groove that travels down the center from base to tip. If your child doesn't have a prominent groove or a "two pack" on that lovely little tongue, start straw drinking. Does his tongue seem wide and/or flat? Is it square at the tip? Is it heart shaped at the tip? Start straw drinking. Can he move the tip from side to side inside his mouth and move foods to the left and the right side with ease? No? Start straw drinking. Can he form a bowl with his tongue, raising the sides just a tad so that the food stays in the central groove? No? Start straw drinking.

Think of your tongue like your arm. The base of the tongue (anchored in your throat) is like your shoulder and provides stability for the rest of the appendage. The blade of the tongue is the arm itself and raises up, lowers or extends thanks to the support of the base, again, just like your shoulder. The lateral margins or sides of the tongue are like your biceps and triceps — tighten those up to show how tough you are or to form a tongue bowl to control the food you are about to swallow. The tip of the tongue is like the hand and fingers. To form a very functional tip, it must extend and contract, just like reaching your arm straight across the table to barely touch the plate of brownies on the other side. Streeettchhh the very tips of your fingers — got 'em! Without that sturdy and unwavering strength in your shoulder, your fingertip could never have snagged that plate of brownies. Likewise, without a strong and stable base of your tongue, the other muscles are not likely to develop to support oral motor skills necessary for accurate articulation and skillful eating.

It's a simple 10-step process to teach your child to drink from a straw independently. Start with a stiff straw that won't collapse if they bite it. Many plastic disposable straw cups come in sets of four cups and four straws. Harder, stiff straws can also be purchased at specialty stores and party goods stores. The straw should be shorter than most, about four- to five-inches-long.

1. Open a full jar of your child's favorite smooth, pureed baby food. Either homemade or store-bought is fine.

2. Dip the straw in the puree and let the tip fill about ½ inch full, so that there is puree inside and outside the straw. Put your finger on the top of the straw to prevent the puree from spilling out the bottom.

3. With your finger still on the top, present the straw and place about ½ inch of the wet

side of the straw flat on you baby's tongue. The straw should be perpendicular to your child's mouth, just like a spoon.

4. Wait for his mouth to close around the puree on the tip, let go of the top hole and then slowly draw the straw straight out of this mouth. The tiny bit of food will be deposited on his tongue for swallowing.

5. Continue with this process until your child can manage a tiny bit more puree inside the straw. The outside of the straw only needs a ½ inch to tempt his little lips to close around the straw.

6. Once your child has mastered steps 1 through 5 (this may take several days of practice) prime the straw with the puree two to three inches from the bottom by sucking on the top and then putting your

finger over the top hole. Dip the bottom of the straw in just ½ inch of the same puree. Note: This can also be accomplished by dipping the straw entirely in the full baby food jar and the wiping off most of the excess before presenting it to your child.

7. Present the straw, wait for lips to close, but don't pull the straw out of his mouth. When you sense that he is ready, lift your finger off the top hole so that the puree can flow. Let him slowly suck and swallow repeatedly until the straw is empty. This step is why it is important to start with purees. Water or thin liquids are just too difficult to manage at first. The puree is just thin enough to flow onto his tongue upon sucking, but not so thin that it is too tricky to manage when all that puree hits his tongue! This is also why I recommend starting with two to

three inches when teaching repetitive sucks (see #6). Moving too quickly to a full straw may startle your little one, and we want this to be an easy, stress-free process.

8. Once your child can manage two to three inches with ease, prime the straw to the top (four to five inches). Practice letting your child suck all the puree through the straw as described in #7.

9. Take the full jar of food, prime the straw as it sits in the jar and add a little dab on the outside of the top hole to tempt him. Hold the jar for him at a 45-degree angle so that the straw enters his mouth as close to perpendicular as possible without spilling and keep it still while he sucks.

10. Once he has learned to drink purees through a straw, gradually thin the puree

with water to nectar consistency and, finally, to liquid consistency. At that point, he is ready to drink thin liquids through a straw.

Note: Wide, short straws with thin liquids require the least amount of effort, but are harder to control when the liquid hits the tongue. Thin, long straws (especially the curly kind!) with purees require the most effort and may be too difficult for some children. Start with a standard width straw (like the kind you get in disposable straw cups with lids), shorten it and use a thin puree, like baby applesauce. Over time, as your child's skill improves, challenge his muscles with the types noted above.

Drinking from a straw creates stronger oral musculature and improves stability during movement of the lips, tongue and jaw. Strength and stability in these structures are essential for eating solids and for talking.

Chapter Seven

What's that Cheerleader Doing in the Swimming Pool?

The Power of Waiting Before Cheering

We have all witnessed it. The shivering three-year-old, dressed in his new Spiderman® swim trunks. Dad is standing waist deep in the local public swimming pool, arms outstretched, shouting "You can do it! There you go! Get your toes on the edge! (Spiderman takes a giant step backwards.) C'mon, just jump! (Spiderman® vehemently shakes his head "NO!") I'll catch you!" and it goes on and on and on. Onlookers pretend not to watch, but carefully wait for the big moment and keep their eyes glued to the edge of the pool, for, at any second, Dad is going to <u>convince</u> his son to jump in! Dad continues to cheer for his little boy, and frankly, if he had pom-poms, he would shake those too! Exasperated, he turns to his wife, who is coaching dad on how to coach his son and standing just a few feet away. Under his breath, dad turns away from junior and focuses his attention on his wife and whispers: "I've been at *this for 20 minutes! When the heck is he going to..." SPLASH! Spiderman® jumps in!*

What just happened there? Johnny got a lot of attention for NOT jumping in the pool. Be careful what you pay attention to... be careful what you reward with your children. Well-intentioned parents and grandparents do this all the time with hesitant eaters in the high chair. "Here comes the airplane... zooom... open up... opennnn uuuuup.... open up for the airplane...now it's flying higher... here it comes." Beware of rewarding your child with attention for <u>not</u> opening up. If your child opens up, the air show ends immediately — and what fun is that?

There is immense power in waiting for a desired behavior to occur. When we cheer constantly for our children, we are reinforcing them for NOT doing it. Instead, try one positive statement to let him know what you are encouraging him to do. The father in the example might say "Put you toes on the blue line by the edge" and wait — about 20 seconds for preschoolers is ideal. Make the statement, wait and praise if it happens. "Your tickly toes are right on that blue line! Yea!" If you wait and it doesn't happen, just state it again: calmly, concisely and consistently. If he takes a step backwards, just wait 20 seconds for him to make the very brave decision on his own or state it again. Once he is on the line and you have praised him, encourage him with a new statement: "You can jump in!" Now wait. After a minute or two, give him a big hug and make a big deal about those tiny toes on the blue line! He'll jump in next time or the next. But, he will make his own decision and feel great about himself if you just encourage and wait.

Praising hesitant eaters follows the exact same course. Try rewarding each step of eating with positive comments, such as:

- "Wow, that roly-poly Brussels sprout almost fell off your spoon, but you made it land on the plate! Good balancing!" This would be appropriate for a child who won't touch the Brussels sprouts, but you suggested he spoon one out of the serving bowl and onto his plate.
- "You can roll those peas across your tray... zoom!" Can't you just envision your little one touching peas for the first time? Touching peas leads to picking up peas, which leads to smelling peas, kissing peas, licking peas, etc.
- "You are a master cruncher! That was loud!" This little girl is being rewarded for

crunching the cracker, even if she can only crunch it between two fingers until she is brave enough to crunch a cracker with her teeth.

- "These rolls smell yummy like Grandma's house... you can smell them too!" That's the perfect amount of praise for a child who decides to finally pick up a roll and give it a whiff.

- "That orange slice looked like a big happy smile when you bit into it!"

- "Hey, where did that asparagus go? In your happy tummy? You're the best at asparagus!"

When we keep each step positive and praise our children for trying, they see themselves as "good eaters" and have the confidence to try again. One of the best phrases I learned from a fantastic mom was "You are such a big-girl eater!" I love that phrase, because you can use it for every stage of learning about food. "You are such a big-girl roly-poly Brussels sprout spoon balancer!" Kids love silly sentences like that!

Make a positive statement and wait for the desired behavior. Reward each step at a time, whether it be learning to ice skate, riding a bike or tasting squash for the very first time.

Chapter Eight

Distraction or Reinforcement?

Sometimes They are One and the Same

One of my favorite clients over the years was a three-year-old little boy who absolutely made me melt... he was that special. His mother, a bright, caring and diligent parent, asked me to teach her little boy to eat purees and drink liquids because he was unable to eat orally for the first three years of his life due to a very rare medical complication. Like many of my little clients, he had a gastrostomy feeding tube that allowed a liquid diet to be pumped directly into his tummy.

The biggest issue? Gabriel gagged and vomited at the slightest touch to his tongue. A sensory obstacle to be addressed in therapy, no doubt. Sure enough, on our first day together, the moment I approached his mouth with his favorite Disney® toothbrush, he gagged. Almost as quickly, his mom leapt onto a stool in the kitchen. Fearing a mouse, I glanced around quickly, gasping and saying suspiciously, "What's wrong?" Mom theatrically jumped down onto the wooden floor and Gabe laughed with absolute pleasure. "Oh, that's what I do every time he gags," Mom said. "It distracts him from vomiting". True, it probably does. But it also accidentally reinforces the gagging. If my mom leapt onto the kitchen stool every time I accidentally gagged, I would quickly become conditioned to gag quite easily! What fun!

Be careful what you reward through distraction. Truly ignore the behavior that you want to fade away and reward or reinforce the behavior that you want your child to continue.

Want to know what we did? We gradually increased the amount of sensory input that Gabe could tolerate on his tongue. He often gagged. We gave the gag very little attention, except to respect his discomfort and wait a minute for him to be comfortable with our approach. Occasionally, he gagged and vomited. We took a towel and covered the vomit and kept going, touching his arm and telling him quietly "You're okay" and only when he was ready, we gently tried again. Over time, his sensitive gag reflex diminished and vomiting ceased.

Feeding therapy for a hypersensitive gag reflex is best addressed with a professional. But, as a parent or caregiver, ask yourself what you are rewarding. Don't give attention to behaviors that are detrimental to progress. Don't smother your child with hugs and kisses every time he takes a little tumble in an effort to distract him from the sudden spill. You'll have a child who is much more tolerant to life's ups and downs if you simply say "You're okay... here we go off to the park!" Give minor falls very little attention. Make it about the destination — the park, or the bite of applesauce.

- I can't say it enough: Be careful what you reward. Ignore the behavior that you want to fade away and reward or reinforce the behavior that you want your child to continue.

Chapter Nine

What's in a Label?

How Our Children Live Up to the Roles

That We Assign to Them

Back in the dark ages, when I worked in the Pediatric Rehabilitation Department at our local community hospital, it was before cell phones, PDAs or text messaging. When I wanted to remember something, I would call my home answering machine from the office and leave myself a message. It typically went something like this: "Melanie, this is Melanie. Don't forget to bring your binder to the meeting tomorrow. Oh, and you looked fabulous today!" My friends in the office would crack up, but I always remembered to check my message machine when I got home because I knew I would hear someone saying something nice about me. Did it really matter that I was talking to myself? It's not like I called myself back. Well, rarely.

Positive statements are the key to working with

kids. Kids live up to the labels that we give them.

"You're so good at licking peas! You're the world's best cruncher... so loud!!!" When we label kids as picky eaters and use phrases in front of them like "Why don't you like them? They are good!" it is like trying to convince a person who is terrified of heights to instantly love sky diving. You might as well be saying "Why don't you want to jump out of a plane from 5,000 feet in the air? It's fun!"

Take it one step at a time when helping a child try new foods. If the best that they can do that day is kiss a green bean, then praise them for puckering up! The next day, they might just make that green bean tap dance across their front teeth. Before you know it, they will taste green beans. If they spit them out, you can still say "Wow, I am really proud of you for trying green beans!" Keep presenting those green beans, don't give up. If they don't learn to like them, that's fine. They don't have to like everything. We just want them to <u>try</u> everything, and helping them to feel good about each step is the key to getting there.

Please don't misunderstand. I am not suggesting that you praise your kids for breathing. I am suggesting that you applaud them for whatever they accomplish that meal — whatever was the most challenging. If your child typically gags at the mere sight or smell of tomatoes, but manages to spoon out one cherry tomato from a serving bowl onto her own dinner plate, then that deserves recognition. "Wow, you balanced that cherry tomato like a circus seal balances a ball! or "You are really good at that — spoons are tricky!"

Remember to model the desired behavior for your kids. Be silly, food is fun! Try to avoid open-ended questions, such as "Can you make your bean tap dance on your teeth?" if you don't want the immediate and most popular answer: "NO!" Try making statements and modeling the fun for them. Grab a bean and work your way up to your mouth. "I love you, you silly bean!" Give it a big smooch. "I can make you tap dance on my teeth! Your bean can tap dance too!" Then laugh and tap dance your way into your child's heart. It's fine to play with your food if the end result is a child who is so interactive with both the food and the others at the table that he proudly tries something that he has never done before. That's the foundation for all learning... experiencing something new.

- Avoid open ended questions if you don't want the answer to be "No!"
- Focus on the positive, even if the best your child could do that day was kiss his peas.
- Affirmative statements such as "Those peas love your kisses!" help your child think of himself as "a good eater" rather a "picky eater."
- Kids live up to the labels that we assign to them. Label your child as a "super cracker cruncher" even if he can only crunch crackers between his fingers. Start small and work up to bigger things one step at a time — your praise for what he CAN do is vital to his growth and development.

Chapter Ten

Dining with the Prison Guards

Monitoring Every Bite Will Come Back to Bite You

One of the most enjoyable aspects of my job is getting to know families, hearing about their careers and interests and teaming together to help everyone have joyful mealtimes. One particular family that I met was interesting to me because both the husband and the wife were security guards. They worked different shifts and had devoted family time between 4 p.m. and 8 p.m. I enjoyed meeting them and watching them play with their five-year-old daughter before dinner was ready. They were both totally engaged and in love with her! Interestingly, the atmosphere shifted the moment everyone sat down at the table. There was practically no conversation except to announce what was for dinner and how much she was expected to eat. The parents watched over her vigilantly as if they were watching the prison mess hall for any signs of mutiny. There was no conversation between the two parents, except to comment on the status of the food on their daughter's plate. When dinner was over, her mother commented on exactly how much she had eaten and her father reprimanded her for not eating her corn...again.

Please understand that these people were wonderful, loving parents. As I got to know them better, I learned that they had both grown up in very commanding households. Their authoritative nature at the dinner table seemed like the right thing to do, yet they knew in their hearts something wasn't working. In *Coping with the Picky Eater* by William G. Wilkoff, M.D., Dr. Wilkoff discusses three types of parenting styles: permissive, authoritarian and authoritative. (3) This family had adopted the authoritarian style only at mealtimes. Dr. Wilkoff notes that for the authoritarian parent, "Rules are many and enforcement is strict". (4) There is no choice in the matter — leaving the child with very little room for independent decision making

While the authoritarian style lies at one end of the parenting spectrum, the permissive parent (otherwise known as the child's best friend) lies at the other. Permissive parents set very few limits. You may recognize this type of parenting style in other chapters in this book. The third style, the authoritative style, lies in the middle of these two extremes. While authoritarian and authoritative may sound alike, the difference lies in the amount of limits that the parent sets. "The authoritative parent has learned enough about children to set limits within which his child can function safely and still have ample opportunity to make decisions for himself." (5)

We want our children to choose to eat a variety of foods with an independent, joyful and healthy approach to mealtimes. One of the key ways to do so is to remember what your role is as the parent. Many parents see themselves as the director or the commander of the household. While we certainly don't want to be overly permissive, we want to strike a balance by setting the stage for our children to make good choices, essentially setting them up for success.

Ellyn Satter's Division of Responsibility Model, described so eloquently in her book *Child of Mine: Feeding with Love and Good Sense*, highlights the parents' and the child's role during snacks and mealtimes. For toddlers through adolescents, "The parent is responsible for *what, when, where of feeding*; children are responsible for *how much* and *whether*." (6) The authoritarian style of parenting interferes with the child's opportunities to learn to make independent choices.

Donna Fish, M.S., L.C.S.W. and author of *Take the Fight out of Food*, wrote an informative chapter on separating our own attitudes about food from our children's eating behaviors. (7) For the family described above, their legacy of being raised in a restrictive household where mealtimes were closely guarded according to how much was eaten and, specifically, which foods were eaten, had trickled down to their young daughter. Over time, they were able to shift their thinking and their demeanor in order for meals to be much more pleasant. A variety of foods were offered, but not monitored bite for bite. Once the dynamic at the table shifted to a more relaxed atmosphere that still had some structure and support for healthy eating, the tension ceased and the child had opportunities to make independent choices regarding what to eat on her plate.

- Mealtimes require structure and family rules, but not so restrictive that parents police every bite of food.
- The parent's job is to present the food during the appropriate meal or snack time in a stress-free environment.
- The child's job is to decide whether to eat it and how much.
- Please refer to www.ellynsatter.com or the resources at the end of this book for more on this topic.

Chapter Eleven

High Chairs are for Eating.

Mommy's Lap is for Her Napkin.

How to Sit in a High Chair Without Fussing

I received a referral to see an 18-month-old who was losing weight. As I drove to his family's apartment, I thought about all of the oral motor delays that I might be observing. But, to my surprise, his oral motor skills were pretty typical for his age. Fortunately, when I arrived, the little guy was hungry and his mother was making him a snack of white rice and noodles in a chicken broth. His mother sat beside the sparkling clean high chair positioned at the end of the dinette table and her little man climbed right up into her lap. He proceeded to have a bite or two, then get down and run about the apartment. To his delight, his mother chased after him! She scooped him up and carried him back to her chair, where she fed him wet noodles and rice for a few more bites until the antics started up again. I glanced at the high chair. "I'd love to see him eat in the high chair," I suggested. "Oh no, he refuses to get in it. He hates it. I always feed him on my lap." With that, the tiny fellow leapt from her grasp and ran into the nearby living room, leaving a trail of wet rice and noodles in case he needed to find his way back to his mother's lap to have another bite.

For the child who is mobile (as in crawling away or running away — the key word is "away") the first step to independent eating is learning to sit and stay in a high chair for up to 20 minutes. For many children, this is a snap! They are content, interested in the finger foods and tolerate some spoon feeding as well. But for other children, it's a challenge to learn to sit and eat when the rest of the world is so darn exciting and ready to be explored... NOW!

The following strategies are essential to learning to stay seated at the table:

1. Keep a regular meal and snack time schedule whenever possible. It should look something like this: breakfast, snack, lunch, snack, dinner, snack, brush teeth and bedtime. Ideally, each meal and snack should be in the high chair and be about two to two-and-a-half hours apart from the beginning of one meal to snack time. Consistency is always the key. As your child improves his attention for eating in the high chair, you can shift your expectations to attending to snack time while the two of you sit together on a bench on the patio. Real life doesn't always allow for every snack or meal in a high chair, but if you can be as consistent as possible at first, you will be pleased with the results.

2. Mark the beginning and end of the meal with a song, a prayer or a ritual that is

special to your family. Children benefit from structure and knowing what is about to happen and when it is over. It might be as simple as saying "Alley OOP! Time to eat!" as you lift your child into his high chair. It is the child's choice to eat while seated at the table. Once he gets down, mealtime is over. Even a toddler can carry his plate to the kitchen counter to confirm that he is done. There is no going back to graze. If the plates are on the counter, we will not be eating again for at least two hours.

3. For preschoolers and older children, you may choose to adopt a rule in your family that everyone stays at the table until the entire family is done eating. Then, the family clears the table together. Younger children may not be able to sit longer than 20 minutes, but should still take their plate

to the kitchen counter before leaving the area to play. If they come back to the table, their plate remains on the counter and you simply comment in this manner if they ask for more food: "Your meal is over because you left the table. We're glad that you came back to visit with us!" Then, engage your child in fun conversation while you continue to enjoy the remainder of your family meal. If he fusses or tantrums, address that behavior as you would during any other time of the day, with a time-out or appropriate consequences.

4. Ask your pediatrician how much liquid, milk or formula your child needs each day. Breastfeeding is not as simple to measure, but be careful with all liquid intake that it does not serve as a meal. If possible, serve filling liquids such as milk at the end of the

meal so as not to fill up tiny tummies before the solid food.

5. Make sure that the child is properly positioned in the high chair (see Chapter 1) for ideal stability and control. Don't forget to use the safety straps consistently. This keeps your child safe and discourages him from getting in and out of the chair.

6. Avoid distractions while eating, such as the television or too many toys. Although it is not a popular belief among many therapists, I allow a small toy at the table as long it facilitates parent/child interaction. For example, I allow a small rubber animal that can be dipped into a new puree while encouraging the child to explore the new taste and texture as he plays and mouths the toy.

7. William G. Wilkoff, M.D., discusses a natural reflex present in most children in his book, *Coping with the Picky Eater*, which is known as the gastrocolic reflex. As little tummies begin to fill, there is a natural urge to have a bowel movement. The request to go potty one time during mealtimes is the exception to steps 1 through 5 above. As the child's body matures, this reflex won't be as active over time. Be sure to give the trip to the bathroom very little attention, and if you must accompany your child, be matter-of-fact about the process. Upon returning to the table together, let the fun begin again!

8. Family meals, whether just the two of you or the entire clan, are meant to be a social occasion! The emphasis is on the time we share together while enjoying the meal, not on the amount that we eat. By following a

regular schedule of meals and snacks offered every 2 to 2½ hours, your child develops a natural hunger cycle and will typically want to eat when seated at the table. After 20 minutes, he will likely be done. If he stays at the table to continue to enjoy the company, that's terrific! If he needs to get down to explore his toy box because he is no longer hungry, that's perfectly acceptable. We will do it all again in about 2 hours!

- Schedule snacks and meals for every 2 to 2½ hours.
- No grazing.
- Mark the beginning and end of each meal with a prayer, song or other family ritual, including taking your plate to the kitchen counter when you are done.
- Limit liquids between meals.
- One potty break during mealtimes.

Chapter Twelve

Famous Courtroom Battles

Tips to Stopping Unnecessary Debates over Food

Joey occasionally will eat fish sticks with some catsup for dipping. As his mother serves him fish sticks for lunch, she keeps her fingers crossed that this will be a day when he won't argue with her. It's especially frustrating because she has witnessed him eating fish sticks every once in a while and he has even asked for more on occasion. However, today is not one of those days. The scene in the courtroom begins something like this.

Joey: (who has dipped the first fish stick in his catsup, abruptly puts it back on his plate.) "I need more catsup!"

Mom: "You have plenty of catsup."

Joey: (louder): "I need more catsup!"

Mom: "Look, you have plenty," pointing at the catsup on his plate.

Joey: "MORE CATSUP!

Mom (exasperated): "Here, look! (abruptly scooping up the fish stick and pushing it in the catsup) Plenty for your fish sticks!"

Joey: "I HATE FISH STICKS!!!"

Once again, Joey, famous trial lawyer, has won. Case closed. Not a fish stick eaten. Court is adjourned.

Some of the best trial attorneys I have ever met are five years old. They are experts in debate. They are masters at convincing their parents that their argument has weight, substance and valuable information as to why they are not eating those fish sticks. But, like all experts in deliberation, the argument is just a diversion. It's not about the catsup — it's about getting your attention over catsup!

Stop engaging. Explain it once and move on. This is the concept behind the single line that our mothers used consistently and concisely whenever a discussion ensued that held no merit: "Because I am the mommy and I said so." Why did that always end the discussion when you were a child? Because your mom said it once and moved on. She didn't engage you in debate because the debate itself only postponed the desired behavior (eating fish sticks) from happening in the first place. You knew that once you heard that reply, there was absolutely no use offering a rebuttal.

Next time you find yourself in this situation, your strategy is to follow the three Cs and be calm, consistent and concise. Let's revisit the scene in the courtroom using the three Cs:

Joey: (who has dipped the first fish stick in his catsup, abruptly puts it back on his plate.) "I need more catsup!"

Mom: (calmly) "When your catsup is all gone, I will be happy to get you more."

Joey: (louder): "I need more catsup!"

Mom does not answer and keeps busy with her back to Joey while she finishes something in the kitchen.

Joey: "MORE CATSUP!

No change in Mom. She is following the three Cs and staying calm, being consistent in her response and being concise if she needs to repeat her response.

Joey: "MORE CATSUP!

Mom replies calmly and does not turn to face him: "When your catsup is all gone, I will be happy to get you more."

Joey begins to dip his fish stick into the catsup.

Mom turns casually to him and says "I'm excited to go to the park with you today. We are going to the one with that really fast slide, right?"

At this moment, this very smart mom is reinforcing Joey's behavior by paying attention to him and engaging him in their exciting plans for the day. She didn't have to say "Good job eating the fish sticks" and definitely not "There! You dipped into the catsup like I asked." Instead, she made the interaction about the two of them and not the food. Please keep in mind that she would not have had this opportunity for enjoying their talk about the park if she did not remain calm, consistent and concise. Likewise, her child would not have had the opportunity to choose for himself to eat the fish sticks without her ability to follow the three Cs.

Please note that this strategy won't change your little attorney's love for debate overnight. He became an attorney at such a young age because it got him lots of attention! Kids love attention from their parents and it is the best reward of all. He will continue to practice law at the dining room table for several weeks while you practice the three Cs.

It is common for children to up the ante by shouting or fussing. If you feel that your child has crossed the line and the behavior has become unacceptable, remove him from the table and his meal is over. A time-out, an immediate loss of a privilege or an age-appropriate method of discipline (not punishment) is in order. Continue to stay calm, consistent and concise and move on.

This short period of testing your ability to follow your own strategy does not mean the three Cs are not working! It means your child is trying everything he can think of to try to stop them from working. As long as you stick to the plan, the negative behaviors (shouting, fussing, etc.) will fade and the desired behaviors (enjoying mealtime with mom and dad, willingness to have other foods on his plate) will increase.

By NOT reinforcing the negative behaviors, but instead allowing them to fade away over time, you have created a more peaceful atmosphere for your child to choose to learn about new foods. And, you have given your child a wonderful gift — a relaxed, enjoyable approach to mealtimes.

- Unnecessary debates distract from the task at hand, which is eating.

- To avoid arguments with your child, don't engage in the debate.

- Follow the three Cs when you respond: Be calm, consistent and concise.

Chapter Thirteen

Just Let Me Know When it's Over!

How to Help your Child Tolerate Tooth Brushing

and Other Daily Routines

"She hates to brush her teeth!" one exasperated mom told me. "I have to literally sit on the floor, wrap my legs around her and brush them. It makes me feel awful and she isn't getting any better about it. Sometimes my husband joins in and finishes brushing them at the end because the whole process is exhausting for me!"

Some kids hate to brush their teeth, to have their hair put in a ponytail or to have their nails clipped. This can be related to sensory integration dysfunction or sensory processing disorder (see Chapter 4) and can also just be a child who doesn't want to cooperate for a variety of valid reasons, including feeling anxious about what is about to happen. Part of their anxiety may also be attributed to not knowing when this experience is going to end.

Kids like predictability, and they quickly learn to trust their parents to provide the guidelines for most tasks. Try singing a song, the same song, every time you brush their teeth, such as "This is the way we brush our teeth, brush our teeth, brush our teeth." You can sing a little faster the first time and gradually sing a little slower as the child learns to tolerate the task. Once the child is more cooperative and tolerating the experience, you can add an extra verse to the song, but be sure to end on the same line, such as "so early in the morning" to signal that you are done. The most important point (and never, never sway from this rule) is that when it is over, it's over. If mommy missed a molar, she doesn't get to go back and brush it if the song is done.

The first day, demonstrate the new routine using a puppet or a doll and your child's toothbrush. Sit your child on a stool near the sink and have her hold the puppet while facing you. Sing the song quickly (be extra silly and fun) and brush the puppet's "teeth" even if it is just a furry, empty mouth! Pronounce "all done!" when you end the song and give the puppet a big hug.

Then, let the child keep holding the puppet to keep their hands occupied and brush the child's teeth. You may not be able to tackle the whole mouth. Start with the area of the mouth that your child tolerates the best. Some children prefer the front teeth and others the sides, where they can feel the back of the toothbrush against the interior of the cheek. I rarely meet a child who prefers the interior edges of the teeth brushed first, although I am sure there are some. The interior of the mouth, which is so close to the throat, is the area the child has a natural instinct to protect, and that is why we have a gag reflex.

For some children, a mirror is helpful, especially if they get to hold it themselves while you do the brushing. Each time you brush, start in the exact same spot and gradually add teeth, one by one, as you sing just a tad slower. It's fine to brush a child's teeth with a soft toothbrush three to four times per day until you slowly but surely increase their tolerance for the entire process.

If you suspect that the toothpaste is the culprit, start with just warm water on the brush. Then, mix a dab of the toothpaste into the cup of water that you dip the brush into as you go so the water is now mildly flavored like toothpaste. Eventually, put <u>less than</u> a pea-sized amount on the brush and spread it across all the bristles, so that a lump of toothpaste doesn't fall off the brush into the child's mouth.

The secret to singing <u>as you brush</u> is that it reinforces the child's cooperative behavior over time. When the child knows that there is a clear beginning and end to the process, their anxiety decreases. Rather than reinforcing the wrestling match by pinning your child to the mat, try reinforcing 10 seconds of brushing with a fun song, a quick hug and trying for 11 seconds the next time. End the process with a big hug and a cheerful "You made it to the end of the song!" or "We brushed three whole teeth... they are so shiny" and repeat the process at least 3 times each day.

- To tolerate tooth brushing, some children needs praise one tooth at a time.
- Try singing the same short song every time you brush his teeth and sing it fast the first time. Then, be done. Over time, you can slow down the song and even add a verse in the middle while gradually increasing his tolerance for tooth brushing.
- Stop singing if he is not cooperative and wait. Start again and be done as quickly as possible, always ending on the same line of the song.
- End the process with a big hug and a cheerful "You made it to the end of the song!"

Chapter Fourteen

"CHOKING!"

Understanding the Signs

Just this year, after 15 years of working with children, I experienced my first true episode of choking. The ironic thing was, it wasn't one of my little clients whom I had to save. I was in a brand new preschool and working with a little girl whom I had previously seen in her home. It was her second day at the school and my first day visiting the classroom. The two teachers in the class of eight toddlers had diligently sat all of the children down at two tiny tables of four, and I sat on the floor beside my sweet client.

As snack was being served and the children had begun eating, the teachers were busy discussing their next activity. I was busy trying to make a good first impression as "a professional" and Emily was busy not eating her snack. While I was entirely focused on engaging with Emily, something made me look up. It wasn't a movement, it wasn't a sound. It was a feeling. The little boy across the table was staring straight ahead, eyes dusky, lips blue and drooling mouth wide open ... but not a sound coming from his throat. The first word out of my mouth was "CHOKING!" in the same way you would scream "FIRE!" (so much for first impressions). In what felt like one deliberate dance of panic, I leapt up from the floor, took two giant steps to reach him, swooped him up and onto my forearm and then flipped him over, ready to deliver four quick back blows. PLOP! Out fell a chunk of food and suddenly he could breathe. Once he settled down and my own heart rate returned to a normal pre-adrenaline thump-thump, I had a minute to reflect on what I just experienced. It was just like they told me in CPR class... choking typically has no sound.

Many parents over the years have anxiously described an uncomfortable eating episode to me as "choking". Upon questioning them further, it's interesting to note that most of the time they mean "gagging" or "coughing" and not choking — which is when the airway is blocked and the child makes no breath sounds and/or very limited vocal sounds. Gagging is a protective mechanism that we are born with and some babies and toddlers have a more sensitive gag reflex than others.

A gag occurs when a bolus of food (or foreign object) triggers an automatic response to prevent the food from going down the throat. Typically, this trigger occurs toward the back of the oral cavity, especially if the soft palate, the arches on the sides of throat or the back of the tongue are stimulated. If you have ever experienced having your throat swabbed for a strep test, you know exactly the spots I am referring to.

When we gag, the soft palate goes up, the jaw thrusts forward and down and the back of the tongue lifts up and forward. Continue to gag and you will likely vomit. But, in between the uncomfortable gags, the child is still able to breathe, cry and, in general, make vocal noises.

Choking typically has no sound, or very intermittent, odd sounds. My point is that when children are learning to eat, we need to keep an eye on them — literally.

The best way to comfort your child when you observe a gag is to firmly touch her arm and say "It's okay...I'm here" and wait, watching her calmly. The gag and cough reflex will likely dislodge the culprit. Don't offer a drink until you are sure the episode is over because fluids can enter the airway during the event. During a gag, never use a finger to grope for the food, as this can push the offending food or object down the throat. An excellent resource for more information on this topic is www.askdrsears.com.

Watch her carefully for any signs of choking, such as any lack of sound, an odd sound that you haven't heard before or a change in color. Be sure that you and any caregivers are certified in CPR and first aid. According to www.askdrsears.com, intervene immediately when you observe any of the following signs:

- Gasping for breath, turning blue
- Fainting (and you suspect choking)
- Displaying an "I'm choking" expression" wide eyes, open mouth, drooling, a panicky look.
- For an older child, showing the universal choking sign by clasping his throat.
- If your child stops breathing, can't cough, or can't make any noise then CALL 911 and try to dislodge the object. (8)

- Be sure that all caregivers for your child are certified in CPR and first aid.
- Choking means the airway is blocked and the child makes no breath sounds or very odd vocal sounds.
- Read the "Entree" above to fully understand the difference between gagging and choking and how to intervene.

Chapter Fifteen

Gimme' Something To Chew!

When, What and How Much to Feed

Recently, I had the unique and incredibly fun experience of producing a children's CD entitled Dancing in the Kitchen: Songs That Celebrate the Joy of Food! *with Joan H. Langford, a popular children's singer and songwriter. The song* Gimme' Something To Chew *is one of my favorites because it is all about a child's confidence as he learns to become an adventurous eater! The song begins this way:*

> *I will eat most anything!*
> *I'll try it once, maybe three times*
> *Go ahead, put it on my plate!*
> *I dare you to give it me, I can't wait!*
> *A ring-a-ding ding, A rooty-toot toot!*
> *Please gimme' gimme' gimme' gimme'*
> *something to chew!*

Knowing when to offer your child new foods, what

to offer and how much to present on their plates

can be confusing between the ages of six months

and two years. Although I highly recommend checking with your child's pediatrician or your family's physician for information on offering solids and table foods after the age of six months, I hope that the following synopsis may simplify it for you.

At approximately 6 months:
Your child may be ready for starter foods, such as pureed fruits and rice cereals. Refer to Chapters 1 and 2 for detailed guidance on how to position your little darling and information on spoon feeding.

At approximately 7 months:
Try smashed or tiny cubes (slightly bigger than a pea) of avocados, mashed potatoes, peaches with the skin removed, carrots, squash, meltable teething biscuits, and pear and apple juice. Acidic fruits such as oranges, grapefruits or tomatoes

can be upsetting to little tummies, so offer those only on occasion. This is the age when tiny fingers are beginning to practice a pincer grasp and cubed soft vegetables are the perfect targets.

Vegetables from low-sodium soups are easy to offer. Meltable cereals sprinkled with water or juice are fun for little fingers! You may notice that he is beginning to bite into soft "biter" biscuits or teething cookies as he develops jaw stability and strength, which indicates that your little guy is moving on to the next stage of oral motor development.

At approximately 8 months:

Strips of cooked fruits or soft raw vegetables such as zucchini strips without the skin are ideal for little fists to grab while new teeth learn to chomp! It's time to introduce pureed or finely ground moist meats, hardboiled egg yolks and different shapes of soft, buttery pasta. Consider the moisture content in the foods. Dry, low-fat ground beef would be difficult for a child this age. Moist, finely ground hamburger (with a slightly higher fat content) in a flavorful sauce will provide a nice introduction to texture and taste, yet is still slippery enough to swallow with ease. The solid food should bind together in the sauce and not be floating in it. It's very difficult for children to manage floating objects in their mouths! Your child is learning to move her tongue to the left and the right or towards the stimulation provided by more textured foods and food strips. When a piece of food is floating in a sauce or a thin puree, her tongue has to manipulate the food and prevent the sauce from spilling down the back of her throat at the same time.

Between 9 and 12 months:

Your little man can bite, chew and swallow dime-sized pieces and strips of soft table foods. Many pediatricians recommend avoiding cow's milk, egg whites, fish, shellfish, nuts and chocolate until at least 12 months of age. Check with your child's pediatrician on these guidelines. Watch carefully that your child doesn't overstuff his mouth. Dole out portions one at a time if you need to assist him with his timing! He is now moving food from the center of his mouth (the doorway) to the sides for immediate chewing, but sometimes he may forget to swallow before allowing another piece in the front door.

Between 12 and 15 months:

Variety is the spice of life! Be sure to offer new foods frequently. In fact, offering a new food 12 to 20 times is vital to helping a child accept new tastes, temperatures and textures. Personally, before I ever became a specialist in this area, I gave up offering new foods to my two toddlers much too quickly! Even if your darling daughter only touches the food, offer it again a day or two later. Offer it again, and again, and again.

According to www.drsears.com, here is what NOT to offer:

- Hard candies
- Nuts and seeds
- Hot dogs (unless cut into pea sized portions or thin, noodle like strips with the skin removed)
- Popcorn
- Whole grapes and raisins
- Olives
- "Globs" of sticky food, such as nut butters; spread all sticky foods thinly on other foods
- Foods that break into solid, hard chunks, such as carrot sticks (9)

After 18 months of age, many children can eat some version of what the rest of the older members of the family are enjoying at mealtimes. Keep in mind that you may need to add moisture to certain foods, such as chicken breast, or cut up larger pieces into thin strips or dime-sized finger foods. Sticky foods, such as nut butters, should be spread thinly on sandwiches and moistened with jelly or cream cheese. Offer sandwiches in strips and snip the edges with scissors one each side, creating a fringe with 1/4 inch between each piece so that tiny dime sized bites tear off of the sandwich with each bite. Alter the foods just slightly to make them more manageable for little mouths and new teeth.

How much food do you offer your child? Well, you might be surprised. According to Dr. Lori Ernsperger in her book, *Just Take a Bite: Easy, Effective Answers to Food Aversions and Food Challenges*, portions of food served in American restaurants "have doubled in size in the last five decades." (10) Americans have lost their perspective of appropriate portion size! Present the portions so that you set your child up for success and don't overwhelm him.

First, select a child-sized plate for any child under the age of five. When trying a new food, a teaspoon of the new food on her plate is a reasonable sampling. An easy guideline that I have learned from dieticians over the years is one tablespoon of food for each year, up to age seven. In other words, most meals include three types of foods. Thus, offer your two-year-old two tablespoons of the meat, vegetable and carbohydrate that you are having for dinner. For snacks, the guideline is the same, but only one food is served along with a drink. For a three-year-old, offer three tablespoons of fish crackers with a few ounces of a beverage.

It's fine to ask you child if she would like more! It's also fine if she doesn't finish the portion you offered. Did you know that the size of your toddler's tummy is approximately the size of her little fist? Yes, it is also true for an adult. Your empty stomach is about the size of your fist.

Chokable Foods:
- Hard candies
- Nuts and seeds
- Hot dogs
- Popcorn
- Whole grapes and raisins
- Olives or round foods like marshmallows
- "Globs" of sticky food, such as nut butters
- Foods that break into solid, hard chunks

Portion sizes up to age 7:
- 1 tablespoon for each year & 3 foods per meal and more if she requests it.
- 1 tablespoon for each year & 1 food per snack. Keep snacks small so that she is hungry for the upcoming meal.

Closing Thoughts

I tease my husband that I have other men in my life. (Of course, they are all under the age of 7.) One little man that will always hold a special place in my heart is Jeremy. In my children's CD, Dancing in the Kitchen, *the first song is titled* Happy Eating Food. *It is truly Jeremy's song. The lyrics are my philosophy on how to approach feeding therapy and speak to the ultimate goal I want all children to know: eating is fun!*

This silly song highlights the funny things that parents have done over the years to celebrate when their children tried new foods. Don't let the lyrics fool you. This is not a song about bribery. Bribery refers to making a deal with your child: "If you do this, then I will do that." Celebrations, however, are social rewards that are spontaneous and reinforce the desired behavior instantly. As parents, we celebrate quite naturally whenever our child acquires a new skill, such as learning to pedal a trike for the first time. When your little one finally figured out how to push just so and make his tiny sneakers rotate those pedals, you probably shouted "Whoo Hoo! You're pedaling!" Did you comment on the fact that the tricycle was veering from one side to the other as the left foot pushed and the right foot pushed back? No, advanced pedaling skills came later and you joyfully rewarded each step as he progressed through Tricycling 101. Eating follows the same course. Step by step, inch by inch, children need reinforcement for their bravery. Celebrate their new skills by being silly! Kids love to know that they can make their parents do silly things. There is nothing more thrilling for children than when their parents turn into great big kids!

In Happy Eating Food, the lyrics go like this: "When you bite one little blueberry, Daddy will dance barefoot in the snow." It's true, Jeremy's Dad did indeed dance barefoot in the snow! He was celebrating Jeremy's success in trying a new food. He was howling up to the moon to proclaim "Jeremy, you are so brave and such a big boy eater!" Jeremy still laughs when he remembers that story and the time that Daddy spontaneously ran out to the backyard in a Colorado snowstorm to let the world know that his son was the reason he was having so much fun. Jeremy was happy eating food!

Jeremy's mom graciously wrote her experiences here for you. I hope that these closing thoughts remind you to take each step to adventurous eating with patience and to celebrate every tiny accomplishment with your child. Thank you for *taking the time to consider my thoughts on the process and for being open to the possibility that mealtimes can be fun, even if you have a picky eater. I wish your family happiness and hope to hear from you at www.mymunchbug.com.*

One Parent's Story

When my son was three years old, he reduced his edible repertoire to two items: French fries and potato chips. At first, as he refused more and more foods, I assumed he was just becoming a "picky eater," like all of my friends' kids did around that age. But before long, his percentiles for weight were sinking faster than the Titanic, and his hair had turned the consistency of steel wool. He also refused to eat in front of peers, or in any situation that was new or otherwise uncomfortable for him. So by the time we got down to the short list of refined potato products, I was in anguish, powerless and walking on eggshells all the time. I read books, I consulted nutritionists and cooks, I tried anything and everything in the world I could possibly think of to get some food down.

Looking back, I am amazed at what developed. Each feeding was a varied combination of presenting the food, waiting, watching, begging, pleading, cajoling, ignoring, bargaining, threatening, waiting some more and then finally giving up. Meal after meal, we both ended up tired, stiff, frustrated and generally upset. Our table time could be up to 1½ hours long—and there were three or more sessions per day! So many opportunities for failure! And hence it was not long before I surrendered to helplessness, and then to hopelessness, and to the certainty that there had never been a parent since the age of the Neanderthals so lacking in skill and maternal instinct.

This was the state of affairs when Melanie arrived at our table. After just a few minutes of observation during dinner, Mel took me aside and offered what I later understood to be her most important words of advice: she told me to relax, to show my son that everything was okay, and to be open to the possibility that eating can be fun. She then instructed me to replace my "worried mommy" face with a "happy" face of both eager anticipation and ease. This was not an easy feat, as I was sure we were on an irreversible path to death by starvation. Yet she assured me that three meals of French fries per day was still a long way from a feeding tube, and a feeding tube was still a long way from death, and so I gradually I began to breathe again. Per Melanie's instructions, I pasted on the "happy" face, and luckily was pretty convincing. And when I saw how my sense of ease in turn relaxed my son, I understood that change for him began with me.

For us, the process was very slow. It took weeks for my son merely to tolerate having a new food sitting on the same plate as the French fries. Then we worked on getting him to touch it, to hold it to his lips, taste it, eat it, and finally to eat it without a major fuss. Expanding his menu required hundreds of tiny steps, a time consuming process to be sure, but one that created many opportunities to celebrate success along the way! In fact, despite his phobic disinclinations, mealtimes gradually became fun times—for all of us. My son's favorite food game was to see what ridiculous thing he could get us to do by trying a new food. Daddy's barefoot ballet in the snow was a sure bet for a big bite!

My son now eats his "three meals a day plus snacks." He is not a perfect eater, but he'll eat from all the food groups, he has regained his percentiles in weight and height, and now will eat at school, in restaurants and even at birthday parties. When he occasionally objects to a food, the hairs still habitually raise up on the back of my neck. But, now I have learned to put on my smirkiest grin, join him in lament for the horror that his life has become, and confirm that he is surely the unluckiest child in the world to have a parent that would serve him this completely inedible mound of so-called food. Then we laugh and move on to another subject while we enjoy each other's company over dinner.

I must also add that with my second child, now six years old, eating was a completely different story, thanks in large part to the tips that Melanie has now shared here in this book. My daughter began eating by feeding herself, making a mess, and delighting in the mealtime process. She still meets new foods with enthusiasm, and eats heartily and healthily. Just last night she declared, "Mom, the asparagus is really, extra delicious tonight!"

Having experienced first-hand the trauma and drama of a child that will not eat, I want to reassure parents that whether your child's challenges are physical or psychological in nature, whether your child is a picky eater or whether you just want to develop healthy attitudes toward eating, it can be done—step by step. Children can learn to eat well, and we can all learn to have fun eating together!

*A final note from Melanie...Shortly after Jeremy
was officially discharged from feeding therapy
(but never from my heart), he sent me this Haiku
in the mail. I still have it on the bulletin board
above my desk because it makes me smile every
single day:*

Lunch
by Jeremy

I like to eat lunch.
All the yummy food we eat.
My lunch. Very great.

Resources

Behavior
Faber A, Mazlish E. *How to Talk So Kids can Learn at Home and in School.* New York, NY: Simon & Schuster; 1995.

Faber A, Mazlish E. *How to Talk So Kids Will Listen & Listen So Kids Will Talk.* New York, NY: Avon Books; 1980.

Frost J. *Supernanny: How to Get the Best from Your Children.* New York, NY: Hyperion; 2005.

Drooling
Marshalla P. *How to STOP Drooling.* Mill Creek, WA: Marshalla Speech & Language; 2006.

Feeding and More
Bahr D. *Nobody Ever Told Me (Or My Mother) That! Everything from Bottles and Breathing to Healthy Speech Development.* Arlington, TX: Sensory World; 2010.

Fraker C, Fishbein M, Cox S, Walbert L. *Food Chaining.* Cambridge, MA: Da Capo Press; 2007.

Morris SE, Klein MD. *Pre-Feeding Skills: A Comprehensive Resource for Mealtime Development*. San Antonio, TX: Therapy Skill Builders; 2000.

Piette L. *Just Two More Bites! Helping Picky Eaters Say Yes to Food*. New York, NY: Three Rivers Press; 2006.

Satter E. *Child of Mine: Feeding with Love and Good Sense*. Boulder, CO: Bull Publishing Co; 2000.

Satter E. *How to Get You Kid to Eat...But Not Too Much*. Palo Alto, CA: Bull Publishing Co; 1987.

Nutrition
Converse J. *Special-Needs Kids Eat Right: Strategies to Help Kids on the Autism Spectrum Focus, Learn, and Thrive*. New York, NY: Penguin Group; 2009

Converse J. *Special-Needs Kids Go Pharm-Free: Nutrition-Focused Tools to Help Minimize Meds and Maximize Health and Well-Being*. New York, NY: Penguin Group; 2010

Picky Eating

Ernsperger L, Stegen-Hanson T. *Finicky Eaters: What to Do When Kids Won't Eat!* Arlington, TX: Future Horizons, Inc: 2005.

Ernsperger L, Stegen-Hanson T. *Just Take a Bite: Easy, Effective Answers to Food Aversions and Eating Challenges.* Arlington, TX: future Horizons, Inc: 2004.

Fish D. *Take the Fight Out of Food: How to Prevent and Solve Your Child's Eating Problems.* New York, NY: Atria Books: 2005.

Wilkoff WG. *Coping with a Picky Eater: A Guide for the Perplexed Parent.* New York, NY: Fireside: 1998.

Sensory Integration

Ayres AJ. *Sensory Integration and the Child.* Los Angeles, CA: WPS: 1994

Miller L. *Sensational Kids: Hope and Help for Children with Sensory Processing Disorder* New York, NY: Penguin Group; 2006

Kranowitz CS. *The Out-of-Sync Child: Recognizing and Coping with Sensory Integration Dysfunction.* New York, NY: A Perigee Book; 1998.

Therapy Techniques
Rosenfeld-Johnson S. *As a Parent What Can I Do?* (DVD). Tucson, AZ: TalkTools; 2008.

Thumb Sucking
Marshalla P. *How to STOP Thumb Sucking and Other Oral Habits*. Mill Creek, WA: Marshalla Speech & Language; 2004.

Web Sites
Ages and Stages, LLC
www.agesandstages.net

American Academy of Pediatrics
www.aap.org

American Occupational Therapy Association
www.aota.org

American Physical Therapy Association
www.apta.org

American Speech Language Hearing Association
www.asha.org

Beckman and Associates
www.beckmanoralmotor.com

International Association of Orofacial Myology
www.iaom.com

Marshalla Speech and Language
www.pammarshalla.com

Mealtime Notions, LLC
www.mealtimenotions.com

New Visions
www.new-vis.com

Nutrition Care
www.nutritioncare.net

Talk Tools Therapy
www.talktools.net

Bibliography

1. Bahr D. *Nobody Ever Told Me (Or My Mother) That! Everything from Bottles and Breathing to Healthy Speech Development.* Arlington, TX: Sensory World; 2010: 22.

2. Ayres AJ. *Sensory Integration and the Child.* Los Angeles, CA: WPS: 1994: 5-6.

3. Wilkoff WG. *Coping with a Picky Eater: A Guide for the Perplexed Parent.* New York, NY: Fireside: 1998: 63-64.

4. Wilkoff WG. *Coping with a Picky Eater: A Guide for the Perplexed Parent.* New York, NY: Fireside: 1998: 63-64.

5. Wilkoff WG. *Coping with a Picky Eater: A Guide for the Perplexed Parent.* New York, NY: Fireside: 1998: 65.

6. Satter E. *Child of Mine: Feeding with Love and Good Sense.* Boulder, CO: Bull Publishing Co; 2000:3.

7. Fish D. *Take the Fight Out of Food: How to Prevent and Solve Your Child's Eating Problems.* New York, NY: Atria Books: 2005: 3.

8. Sears W, Sears M. *Childhood Illnesses: Choking 101.* http://www.askdrsears.com. Accessed October 11, 2010.

9. Sears W, Sears M. *Chokable Foods.* http://www.askdrsears.com. Accessed October 11, 2010.

10. Ernsperger L, Stegen-Hanson T. *Finicky Eaters: What to Do When Kids Won't Eat!* Arlington, TX: Future Horizons, Inc: 2005: 122.